SALTWATER CROCODILE

by Rachel Rose

Minneapolis, Minnesota

Credits

Cover and title page, © miralex/Getty Images; 4–5, © David Curl/Minden; 7, © David Wall/Alamy; 8–9, © CMH Images/Alamy; 10–11, © Johan Larson/Shutterstock; 12–13, © Lauren Suryanata/Shutterstock; 14–15, © Chris Putnam/Alamy; 16–17, © PomInOz/Shutterstock; 18, © Supermop/Shutterstock; 18–19, © Nibaphoto/Alamy; 20–21, © Bernard Radvaner/Getty Images; 22, © DianaLynne/iStock.

Bearport Publishing Company Product Development Team

President: Jen Jenson; Director of Product Development: Spencer Brinker; Managing Editor: Allison Juda; Associate Editor: Naomi Reich; Associate Editor: Tiana Tran; Art Director: Colin O'Dea; Designer: Elena Klinkner; Designer: Kayla Eggert; Product Development Assistant: Owen Hamlin

STATEMENT ON USAGE OF GENERATIVE ARTIFICIAL INTELLIGENCE
Bearport Publishing remains committed to publishing high-quality nonfiction books. Therefore, we restrict the use of generative AI to ensure accuracy of all text and visual components pertaining to a book's subject. See BearportPublishing.com for details.

Library of Congress Cataloging-in-Publication Data

Names: Rose, Rachel, 1968- author.
Title: Saltwater crocodile / by Rachel Rose.
Description: Minneapolis, Minnesota : Bearport Publishing Company, [2024] | Series: Danger down under | Includes bibliographical references and index.
Identifiers: LCCN 2023032873 (print) | LCCN 2023032874 (ebook) | ISBN 9798889164982 (library binding) | ISBN 9798889165057 (paperback) | ISBN 9798889165118 (ebook)
Subjects: LCSH: Crocodylus porosus--Juvenile literature.
Classification: LCC QL666.C925 R67 2024 (print) | LCC QL666.C925 (ebook) | DDC 597.98/2--dc23/eng/20230804
LC record available at https://lccn.loc.gov/2023032873
LC ebook record available at https://lccn.loc.gov/2023032874

Copyright ©2024 Bearport Publishing Company. All rights reserved. No part of this publication may be reproduced in whole or in part, stored in any retrieval system, or transmitted in any form or by any means, electronic, mechanical, photocopying, recording, or otherwise, without written permission from the publisher.

For more information, write to Bearport Publishing, 5357 Penn Avenue South, Minneapolis, MN 55419.

CONTENTS

Death Roll 4
Salty or Not? 6
The Biggest and Baddest 8
Hide and Seek 10
Top Croc 12
Chow Time 14
Watch Out! 16
Tiny Chirps 18
Stayin' Alive 20

More about Saltwater Crocodiles 22
Glossary 23
Index 24
Read More 24
Learn More Online 24
About the Author 24

DEATH ROLL

There's danger lurking in the waters Down Under!

A big beast lunges out of a river, grabbing a surprised snake and dragging it beneath the surface. The saltwater crocodile holds its **prey** underwater and spins around again and again. The death roll finishes the creature off. Australia's **fierce** crocodile begins to feast!

! Saltwater crocodiles are also known as salties.

SALTY OR NOT?

Saltwater crocodiles have a huge **range**. Some live in the coastal waters off eastern India and Southeast Asia, but many salties make their homes along the northern coast of Australia. As their name suggests, these crocs are usually found in saltwater. They can also live in some freshwater **habitats**, such as rivers, lakes, and inland swamps.

> These crocs can spend days, and sometimes weeks, out at sea.

THE BIGGEST AND BADDEST

These crocs are the biggest **reptiles** on Earth. From their noses to their tails, **male** salties can grow to be 23 feet (7 m) long. That's about as long as a small school bus! **Females** tend to be smaller, usually growing to only about half the size of males.

!

Male salties can weigh more than 2,200 pounds (1,000 kg). That's as heavy as a small car.

HIDE AND SEEK

Despite their huge size, salties are sneaky **predators**. Their bodies are made for lurking below the water. The animals' dark green and brown coloring helps them blend in with the murky bottom. Their eyes, ears, and **nostrils** are on the top of their big heads. This allows the crocs to breathe, see, and hear while hiding almost completely underwater.

Saltwater crocodiles can also stay entirely underwater for a long time. They can hold their breath for up to eight hours.

TOP CROC

These crocs are so mighty, there aren't any creatures that dare to hunt them. This makes them **apex predators**. And being unmatched comes in handy when the crocs are hungry. Salties will eat almost anything they can sink their teeth into, including fish, kangaroos, and water buffalo. When something tasty appears, the crocs leap out of the water in a a surprise attack!

! Most salties have 66 teeth. Each tooth can grow up to 5 inches (13 cm) long.

A saltie eating a large fish

CHOW TIME

Saltwater crocs chomp down hard on their prey. *Snap!* These fierce predators have the strongest bite force of any animal on Earth. Salties don't let go as they drown their catch underwater. If the meal is large, the crocs spin violently with the prey still tightly in their mouths. This death roll breaks the meal into smaller pieces. Smaller prey is often swallowed whole.

Although they can close their mouths with a lot of power, salties don't have much strength to open their mouths back up.

A saltie using the death roll

WATCH OUT!

Salties don't attack humans often, but it can still happen. It's important to be extremely careful if you're in places where these crocs live. They make their homes in water, but they also spend a lot of time on land, getting warm in the sun. And they move faster than you'd think— salties can reach 14 miles per hour (22 kph) in a matter of seconds. So watch out!

Human hunters were once the biggest threat to salties, but the animals have been safer since Australia banned crocodile hunting in 1971.

TINY CHIRPS

Crocs **mate** in the spring. Then, the female crocodile swims for inland waters where she makes her nest on a river's edge. She lays up to 70 eggs before covering them with plants and mud. After about 90 days, the babies **hatch**. They begin to make a chirping sound so their mom knows it's time to dig them out.

! Baby salties are about 1 ft (30 cm) long when they hatch.

STAYIN' ALIVE

The mother croc looks after her babies, but life is still tough for the new crocodiles. Small salties are often eaten by bigger animals, such as birds and snakes. Many of the babies don't live long enough to become adults. But those that do grow up are soon big and strong. Watch out for this danger Down Under!

Adult saltwater crocodiles can live for about 65 years.

MORE ABOUT SALTWATER CROCODILES

⚠ There are about 500,000 saltwater crocodiles in Australia.

⚠ Saltwater crocodiles often spend their days warming up in the sun and their nights hunting.

⚠ Crocodiles can keep their mouths open under the water without swallowing any.

⚠ Like all crocodiles, salties can sleep with one eye open.

⚠ Like all reptiles, salties aren't able to sweat. Instead, they cool off by panting through their mouths.

⚠ A female crocodile is called a cow. A male is called a bull.

GLOSSARY

apex predators animals that are not killed by any other animals

females saltwater crocodiles that can lay eggs

fierce very dangerous and violent

habitats places in nature where animals normally live

hatch to break out of an egg

male a saltwater crocodile that cannot lay eggs

mate to come together to have young

nostrils openings in the nose that are used for breathing and smelling

predators animals that hunt and eat other animals

prey animals that are hunted and eaten by other animals

range the region throughout which a kind of animal naturally lives

reptiles cold-blooded animals that have dry, scaly skin, a backbone, and lungs for breathing

Index

color 10
death roll 4, 14–15
eggs 18
female 8, 18, 22
habitats 6
humans 16
jaws 14
male 8, 22
mouth 14, 22
nest 18
predators 10, 12, 14
prey 4, 10, 14
teeth 12–13

Read More

Emminizer, Theresa. *Saltwater Crocodile: The Largest Reptile (Animal Record Breakers).* New York: PowerKids Press, 2020.

Markle, Sandra. *On the Hunt with Crocodiles (Ultimate Predators).* Minneapolis: Lerner Publications, 2023.

Learn More Online

1. Go to **www.factsurfer.com** or scan the QR code below.
2. Enter "**Saltwater Crocodile**" into the search box.
3. Click on the cover of this book to see a list of websites.

About the Author

Rachel Rose writes books for kids and teaches yoga. Her favorite animal of all is her dog, Sandy.